CCSS **Genre** Realistic Fict

Essential Question
How do we get the things we need?

by Anna Kenna
illustrated by Diane Palmisciano

Chapter 1

Dogs Rule!

Jamila walked in, closed the front door, and dumped her backpack on the kitchen counter. "Hi, Mom," she called.

"Hi, honey," her mom replied over the drone of the clippers. It wasn't hard to guess that her mom was working—as usual.

When Jamila entered the laundry room, her mom was clipping a large black poodle. "Hi, Alfred," said Jamila in a friendly voice as she tickled the dog under the chin. Like most of her mom's customers, Alfred didn't look too pleased about being groomed.

Jamila's mom was a professional dog groomer. She used to work at a dog-grooming salon, but when that closed, she set up a business at home. "It'll only be for a couple of months," she'd told Jamila. That was a year ago!

Jamila's mom switched off the clippers. "So how was your day?"

"I slayed a dragon that was rampaging through the school bus, wrestled a python in the library, and had another call from Hollywood," replied Jamila.

Her mom smiled. "Just a regular day, then?"

"Totally," said Jamila.

Her mom picked up the scissors. "Almost done here. There's some yogurt and fruit in the refrigerator."

As Jamila was scraping out the last of the yogurt from the container, there was a knock on the door, and she opened it to find a tall man with dark curly hair standing there. "I've come to get Alfred," he said.

"Sure," said Jamila. "Come in."

Jamila was used to the comings and goings of dog owners. They were always dropping off or picking up dogs. You could even see the path they'd worn across the grass.

After he left, Jamila's mom came in. "Whew, I feel as if I've been wrestling a python myself," she said as she took off her apron and flopped into a chair. "That Alfred is a real handful."

Jamila thought her mom looked tired. Her hair was scooped into a loose ponytail, and there were dark shadows under her eyes. "How many dogs today?" Jamila asked.

"Let's see," said her mom, sighing as she tucked a stray hair behind her ear. "There were Wilma and Fred this morning. You know those two Yorkshire terriers? Brodie was after lunch, then that crazy cocker spaniel, Lucy, and now Alfred."

Alfred

Wilma

Fred

Lucy

Brodie

"Right," said Jamila. She could see why her mom looked so worn out! Even after the last dog had left for the day, her work wasn't finished. She'd always rush around, scrubbing out the tub, sweeping hair off the floor, and spraying air freshener all around.

"I'm so over this," she'd often say. "I can't wait for the day we have our house to ourselves."

Jamila knew her mom dreamed of moving her business out of the house, but she couldn't see it happening anytime soon because that would be expensive.

And although her mom was skilled at dog grooming, Jamila knew that it wasn't like earning regular wages—business could get slow, and money could get scarce. Right now, however, Jamila's mom was in the middle of the busiest time of the year. The county dog show was coming up, and all the dog owners wanted their pooches to look their best.

"Don't forget that Melissa's coming after school tomorrow," said Jamila as her mom put the broom and dustpan away. "We're going to work on our science project together."

"Yes, I remember," said her mom. "But just warn her that I'll be working, okay?"

"She knows," said Jamila. "I told her the dog show's on."

Her mom yawned. "Okay, what are we going to have for dinner? Did I hear you say something about a dragon casserole?"

Chapter 2
Canine Chaos

The next day, Jamila and Melissa arrived home from school to the familiar hum of dog clippers. "Hi, Mrs. J.," said Melissa, poking her head around the door.

"Hi, Melissa," said Jamila's mom. "Meet last year's Supreme Grand Champion. His name is Bob."

"Hello, Bob," said Melissa, giggling as a small white fluff ball with a wrinkled face blinked its bulging eyes at her.

The girls set up their science project on the kitchen table. They were testing the gluten content of different types of flour. Jamila set three bowls and a jug of water on the table. Next, she carefully put a spoonful of flour into each bowl.

There was a knock at the door. "I'll get it," Jamila's mom yelled. "Bring him in, Mrs. Cruz," they heard her say.

The girls heard loud panting and the soft thud of paws, and suddenly a huge brown dog burst into the room. He looked like a woolly mammoth, without the tusks, and was towing a thin woman at the end of a long leash.

"Oh, my goodness," said Jamila's mom. "Just a moment, I'll ..." It was too late. The huge animal bounded onto the table, one of his massive paws landing in a bowl of flour. With a yelp, he skidded across the table, sent the other bowls flying, and landed on top of Melissa.

"I am so sorry, girls," Jamila's mom kept saying as she helped them clean up the mess. Melissa's clothes were caked with a sticky paste, she had a smudge of white flour on her cheek, and her notebook was soaking wet. Floury pawprints led to a cage in the hallway where the culprit now whimpered pitifully.

"It's okay," said Melissa, smiling sweetly. "Honestly."

But Jamila wasn't prepared to risk setting up the experiment again. "Maybe we'll do it at your place tomorrow," she suggested to Melissa while looking pointedly at her mom. A short time later, Melissa left.

That night when Jamila was getting ready for bed, her mom came in. "Honey, I'm so sorry about what happened today," she said.

Jamila looked at her mom. She still had her apron on, her dark hair was dusted with flour, and she looked really upset. Jamila couldn't help herself. Her serious look changed to a grin. "Actually, it was pretty funny," she said.

Her mom sank onto the bed and grinned sheepishly. "What a fiasco. I call that dog the yeti, and now you know why!" They both laughed until tears were rolling down their faces.

Jamila's mom wiped her eyes and suddenly looked serious. "Today made me realize one thing," she said. "This just can't go on. It's not fair to you, and it's really getting me down."

"It's okay, Mom, really," said Jamila.

"It's not," said her mom firmly. "When the dog show is over, I'm going to the bank to apply for a loan to set up my own dog-grooming salon. With the number of regular clients I've built up, I hope they'll see my business as a good investment."

Jamila knew that it would be difficult to get a loan from the bank, but she loved seeing her mom so excited about her business. One way or another, she knew her mom would figure out how to make this work.

Chapter 3
The Name Game

The next two weeks were busier than ever with dogs coming and going from morning until night. Since the yeti incident, the front of the house was out of bounds to dogs, and Jamila's mom put up a sign telling clients to bring their dogs around to the side door.

One afternoon, Jamila's mom said she had something to show her. "Come on," she said. "It's not far." They jumped into the car, and after a short drive, they pulled into the parking lot of a small strip mall.

"See that place there?" said her mom, pointing to a vacant store between a restaurant and a dry-cleaning shop. "It would be perfect for a dog-grooming salon. It needs some walls knocked down and some plumbing work, but it's a good possibility."

"Did the bank give you a loan?" asked Jamila.

Her mom shook her head. "First, I have to estimate how much everything will cost. It's turning out to be more expensive than I thought, but we'll see."

Jamila's mom was in a good mood for the rest of the week, and on Friday night, they went to their favorite restaurant for dinner.

"We'll have to think of a name for the salon," said Jamila's mom as they waited for their order.

"Cool," said Jamila. She grabbed a napkin and borrowed her mom's pen. By the time they'd finished eating, they had made quite a list: Hound Heaven, Pooch Parlor, Canine Clippers, Paws 'n' Claws.

"We're great at this," said Jamila, passing the napkin to her mom. "Maybe we should open an advertising business instead."

🐾 🐾 🐾 🐾

The week after the dog show, Jamila arrived home to find her mom sitting at the dining table instead of running around like usual. Jamila knew right away that something was wrong.

"No loan?" she asked.

"No loan," her mom replied.

She explained that the bank manager had been very nice and really wanted to help, but he couldn't take the risk of offering her the size of loan she would need.

"I'm sorry, Mom," said Jamila. She gave her mom a hug and then made two strawberry smoothies. For a while, they sat in silence, sipping their drinks. Finally, Jamila asked, "So, does that mean our cool salon names are wasted?"

"Not wasted," said her mom, "just on hold for the moment, I guess."

As she said that, Jamila noticed her mom's face suddenly change. Her eyes had become focused, and she was sitting up straighter. "What is it?" Jamila asked.

"I've just had an idea," said her mom. "I don't know why I didn't think of it before." She rushed into her bedroom to make a phone call, leaving Jamila staring after her.

As Jamila noisily sucked the last of her smoothie, her mom came out of her bedroom with a huge smile. "We're going for a drive on Saturday," she said, but no matter how hard Jamila quizzed her, she wouldn't say where.

Chapter 4
A Mystery Journey

On Saturday, Jamila and her mom headed off on the freeway. Her mom was singing along to the radio. Jamila hadn't seen her so happy in ages.

An hour out of town, they took an exit and were soon driving past fields of tall crops. After a few bumpy miles along a dirt road, they turned in to a farm gate. As they pulled up, a woman came out to greet them.

"Pam, you're looking fantastic!" said Jamila's mom as the two hugged each other.

"This is Jamila," said her mom.

"Hi, Jamila," the woman said. Her face crinkled pleasantly as she smiled.

While Pam went to get some keys, Jamila's mom explained that she used to work for Pam and her husband and that they'd taught her all she knew about dog grooming. Later they sold their dog-grooming salon and ran a mobile business until they retired last year.

They followed Pam to a garage where she lifted the door to reveal a large van with a picture of a well-groomed dog on the side. Slowly it dawned on Jamila what her mom wanted to do. "Oh, I get it," she said, and they all laughed.

On the way home, Jamila's mom explained that Pam had agreed to sell the van to her and let her pay it off out of her profits. "And the bank has agreed to a small loan for the setup costs," she said. "So, we can afford this without dipping into our savings."

"But how did you know about the van?" asked Jamila.

"I knew Pam and her husband had retired," her mom said. "I just hoped they hadn't sold the van yet."

"It's very generous of them to help you out," said Jamila.

"They've always been mentors to me," her mom explained. "I think they just want to see me do well."

A week later, Pam and her husband delivered the van. They also gave Jamila's mom a list of their old clients and some leftover bottles of dog shampoo.

"May you prosper with this old van, my dear," said Pam.

"Yes," her husband added. "We wish you the very best. It's great that the vehicle's going to be used again."

After Pam and her husband left, Jamila and her mom climbed inside the vehicle. There was a big bathtub, a grooming table, and lots of storage space for all the lotions and potions that cluttered their laundry room.

"Isn't it great?" said Jamila's mom, smiling.

"It sure is," said Jamila, easing herself into the tub. "But I wonder if you'll get the yeti in here."

Jamila's mom clasped her hands with excitement. "We've still got to choose a name for the business," she said. "Where's that list we made?"

"Don't need it," said Jamila. "I've come up with something even better."

"Right, let's hear it," said her mom.

Jamila tapped out a pretend drum roll on the side of the tub. "Can-do Canines," she said. "What do you think?"

"Can-do Canines?" Her mom repeated the phrase, rolling it around on her tongue. "Brilliant," she said, throwing her arms around Jamila. "Can-do Canines! I absolutely love it."

Respond to Reading

Summarize

Use important details from *Can-do Canines* to summarize the story. Your graphic organizer may help you.

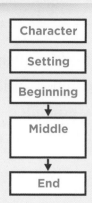

| Character |
| Setting |
| Beginning |
↓
| Middle |
↓
| End |

Text Evidence

1. What kind of fiction is this story? How can you tell?
GENRE

2. What events in Chapter 3 led Jamila's mom to try to get a loan from the bank? **SEQUENCE**

3. What does *investment* on page 9 mean? Use clues in the sentence to help you figure it out.
SENTENCE CLUES

4. Write about the sequence of events that led to Jamila's mom finding a solution to her problem.
WRITE ABOUT READING

Compare Texts

Read to find out how banks help people get what they need.

You Can Bank on It

Banks help people to buy homes and start businesses. In *Can-do Canines*, Jamila's mother asked the bank for a loan to help her realize her dream of setting up her own dog-grooming salon.

Making Money

When you deposit money in a bank, the bank pays you interest. The longer you leave the money in an account, the more interest it earns. Say you put $1,000 in the bank, and you are offered 3 percent interest every year. After a year, it will be worth $1,030. The $30 is the interest the bank pays you to use your money.

Making a Profit

Banks are businesses too. Every business needs to earn a profit. A profit is the money you make after you have paid all your costs. Banks earn a profit by borrowing money from some customers and lending it to others. They pay to borrow money but charge more to lend it. The difference is the profit.

On the other hand, if you borrow money from a bank, you have to pay the bank for the use of that money. This fee is also called interest.

Darren Greenwood/DesignPics

Starting a Business

Most new businesses need to borrow money to get started. The obvious place to go for a loan is a bank.

In *Can-do Canines*, Jamila's mom asked the bank for a small loan to set up her salon. Like most new businesses, a mobile dog-grooming salon would have some start-up costs. For example, Jamila's mom would need to pay for advertising and to purchase grooming products. Let's say all this cost around $10,000. If the bank loans her that money, it will charge her interest on the loan.

A bank teller serves a customer.

Charging Interest

Imagine Jamila's mom takes out the $10,000 loan for five years, and the bank charges 5 percent interest on the loan every year. At the end of five years, Jamila's mom will have to pay the bank $12,500.00. The extra $2,500.00 is the fee she will pay the bank for lending her the money.

(bkgd) Darren Greenwood/DesignPics, (br) Ryan McVay/Photodisc/Getty Images

Thanks to changes in technology, people can do their banking without having to leave home.

Keeping Your Money Safe

The idea of banking is believed to have started thousands of years ago. It's thought that in ancient times, temples were kinds of banks. People used them as places to keep gold and other valuable goods.

Banks are continually changing. Today, many people use plastic cards instead of cash. You can withdraw money using a cash machine, and you can do most of your banking online. In fact, there are some banks you can't visit because their services are only available online. Even though banks have changed a lot over thousands of years, they're still the safest place to keep your money.

Make Connections

How do banks help people get what they need?
ESSENTIAL QUESTION

What did you learn from both texts about the ways banks help businesses? **TEXT TO TEXT**

(bkgd) Darren Greenwood/DesignPics, (tl) Ariel Skelley/Riser/Getty Images

Focus on
Literary Elements

Similes Similes are figures of speech that compare two things by using the words *like* or *as*. For example, *busy as a bee* means very busy.

Read and Find On page 6 in *Can-do Canines*, Jamila describes the dog as looking "like a woolly mammoth." This means that the dog has a thick coat of long fur.

Your Turn

Find a scene in the story *Can-do Canines* that includes at least one description. Rewrite the scene, replacing the description with a simile. See if you can rewrite more than one description with a simile.